Good Morning Sunshine!

FINDING STRENGTH AND COMFORT IN GOD

God is good!

Terri L. Braun

Terri L. Braun

ISBN 978-1-64028-120-2 (Paperback)
ISBN 978-1-64028-121-9 (Digital)

Christian Faith Publishing, Inc.
296 Chestnut Street
Meadville, PA 16335
www.christianfaithpublishing.com

Printed in the United States of America

To Ray Dean Courtney, who taught me that life isn't easy or fair and to always look up because God is always there. I miss you, Dad.

Introduction

I was thirty-two years old when my dad was called into God's care. He suffered an aneurysm to the brain at the young age of fifty-four. Although I didn't get to say good-bye, his memories live vividly in my heart. To those who had the privilege of knowing him, he was a breath of fresh air. He was the very epitome of serving others. His positivity and bright outlook on life were hard to emulate. In my eyes, he was all that was good in the world, and I was honored to be able to call him dad. He is missed dearly but has continued to smile upon my heart as this book was created in his memory.

My favorite memory of him is the same one that annoyed me the most as a child! If anyone knows me, they know that I am *not* a morning person (I have mastered that "don't talk to me yet" glare). Each morning, my dad would come bouncing into my room, all cheerful with his wonderful toothy smile, and, while annoyingly flipping the lights off and on, would say, "Wake up, sunshine. It's morning." I would drag myself out of bed, get dressed, and go to the kitchen where he dared to still be smiling. Even though I would give him my best morning glare, he would still say, "Good morning, sunshine." This simple phrase, those three little words, had so much power behind them and has become my philosophy through life. They made me realize that not only is each day a new day to celebrate but that I could also shine through all of the struggles of the day by finding the "sunny" parts. It also encouraged me to be the sunshine for someone else's day.

In all his earthly wisdom, he also used to warn me that life would be hard and that "the sooner you realize life isn't fair, the easier it will be." He was right because on the day of June 21, 2014, life became very unfair. On that windy day, I was passing by a basketball goal, and a strong gust of wind blew it over, landing it on my head and knocking me unconscious. Thus, I suffered a traumatic brain injury and have struggled through several years of therapy and rehabilitation. Somewhere along my journey, I forgot everything Dad taught me. I forgot to find the sunny parts of my day and forgot that I could face adversity because God blesses us with a new day every day. I forgot that valuable lesson that life wasn't fair, and I fell into the trap of self-pity, which led to depression and anxiety.

I watched myself spiral into a pit of despair where my world became so dark. I began to hate God for the daily struggles I had to endure. I tried many things that I thought would lift me up and give me hope again, but they all failed. I soon realized that the only one who could save me from my own destructive thoughts and raise me out of the darkness was God. Every day, I devoted myself to reading his Word, and I began to cherish my relationship with him and looked forward to spending time with him. As my relationship with God deepened, I found that the sunshine seemed to become brighter, the clouds began to part, and the darkness faded.

After what seemed like a lifetime, I began to enjoy life once again, and my dad's words rang in my ears. I remembered that when that sunshine begins peaking up out of the horizon, there is new hope and that each day is a gift from God. Now when I wake up, I lift my head off the pillow, give thanks to God for another day, look out my window, and say, "Good morning, sunshine," just as my dad used to say to me.

There are many lessons I have learned over the last two-and-a-half years of recovery. Through reading his Word daily, I found strength and comfort. I have chosen forty verses that have lifted me up and shared how they helped me through my daily struggles. I hope that through them you can also find the peace and happiness that God wants for every one of us.

God is calling us forward, not backward. Put the days of past hurt and heartache behind you. Don't listen to that little voice of doubt that says you can't face the day. This is not God's voice but your own. His voice is encouraging, loving, and inspiring. He wants you to face each day with courage. He does not want you to dwell on your past mistakes or your past ways. The past cannot be redone, and all those mistakes have been forgiven. God doesn't wish for you to live in the past. He simply wants you to learn from your experiences. He sees wonderful qualities in you and is calling you to follow him. He sees your full potential, even when you don't see it in yourself. He sees the person who can do his will and make the world a better place. You are only human, and he doesn't expect perfection from you; Jesus was the only one who walked the earth who was perfect, without sin. Look at your weaknesses and mistakes and use them to grow in your faith. God must be the center of your life, so take time daily for prayer, reflection, and contemplation of how you can move forward to a deeper relationship with God. Those that follow him will find a peace and contentment in each new day.

Reflection Questions

1. Do you let your past influence what you do today?
2. Is talking to God a priority in your life?
1. What would you accomplish as you reach the full potential of being a child of God?

> *"My grace is sufficient for you, for power is made perfect in weakness." I will rather boast most gladly of my weaknesses, in order that the power of Christ may dwell in me. Therefore, I am content with weaknesses, insults, hardships, persecutions, and constraints, for the sake of Christ; for when I am weak, then I am strong. (2 Corinthians 12: 9–10)*

Carry your cross, your burdens, your troubles, and your ailments respectfully and gratefully. Jesus carried all our sins to the cross. Our sins put him on the cross, but his love for us kept him there until death. He felt the weight of every person's sin hanging on that cross. Imagine the pain and agony he must have felt. He died for every single one of us so that we can go to heaven. Sometimes the struggles you face every day blinds you of his love, and you get caught in the trap of self-pity. You start feeling sorry for yourself and questioning God, "Why me?" You may think no one understands your troubles and that you are alone. Open your eyes, pick yourself up, and remember God is always with you. There is no reason to pity yourself, as you have something wonderful and freeing within your grasp. Just reach out and look up. By choosing God over self-pity, you have now opened new opportunities for your mind and soul to grow. Every struggle you face helps to define you. It helps you to gain strength and compassion for others. If you choose to do so, you can be a vessel to help others, as you can empathize with those that have the same struggles. Nurture your relationship with God, cherish it, and spend time every day in prayer. Every day you must be grateful and thankful. You will begin to see that you will find strength in your weaknesses and that you are strongest when you are the weakest.

Reflection Questions

1. Do you feel sorry for yourself because of your struggles?

2. Do you let self-pity rob you of participating in life?

3. Have you reached out to someone who is experiencing the same difficulties?

> *And let the peace of Christ control your hearts, the peace into which you were also called in one body. And be thankful. (Colossians 3:15)*

Leave the past in the past and don't stumble on the things that are behind you. Your mistakes do not define who you *can* be. Make today be the day you "start over" with God by your side. Give yourself fully to him. Trust that he will provide for you and that he is in control. God has already forgiven yesterday's sins. Why should you hang onto them if he hasn't? Do you believe that you know better than him? The more you try to take control, the more frustrated you will become. When you try to control life, it starts falling apart, and you will feel alone and afraid; but if you believe that God is in control, you will find pieces starting to fall into place. He believes that there is so much good in you and that you are worth so much to him that he gave his only son up for you. So don't be self-sufficient, rely on him. Lean on him during those times of struggle when you feel alone. You are never alone, as God is always with you. Trust in him, even when you don't understand, that his will is what is best. Give him control, as only he knows what tomorrow will hold. You can count on one thing for certain—that he will give you peace today, tomorrow, and eternity. Let him.

Reflection Questions

1. Is God the first one you turn to when you feel everything falling apart?

2. How often during the day do you try to control your circumstances?

3. Do you truly believe that God is in control?

> *Then he said to all, "If anyone wishes to come after me, he must deny himself and take up his cross daily and follow me. For whoever wishes to save his life will lose it, but whoever loses his life for my sake will save it." (Luke 9:23–24)*

Some days you may not want to face the hardships and wonder what the purpose of the pain is. Remember that your true destination is with God in heaven. Life is a journey on earth, a pilgrimage. It is your journey and doesn't have to be full of pain; it can be a wonderful journey should you decide to listen and learn from God's Word. God never said that life would all be good times and no hard times. He never said that you won't encounter hardships and struggles. In fact, it is just the opposite. He said you are to take up your own cross daily. By taking up your cross and handling your problems with dignity and grace, you will find an inner happiness and contentment that only he can provide. Learn to keep God close to you through the good times, for it is easy to forget him when everything is going your way. And do not abandon him during the rough times, as it is easy to think that he isn't there for you. At times, you may even to begin to hate him for what you endure. Follow him every day and serve him. You will be fulfilled and suddenly see the purpose of life. Instead of just drifting aimlessly on this earth, you will have a path to follow. We are not all called to do great things; sometimes it is to do small things in great ways, says St. Mother Theresa. So serving others, loving others, and helping those less fortunate are something we must do daily to serve God. Choose to be kind and be patient with yourself and others. To have peace on earth, you must believe that you are called to serve him so that your journey on earth will lead you home.

Reflection Questions

1. Do you get mad at God for your struggles and challenges in life?

2. Do you know what your purpose on this earth is?

3. Are you always complaining to others about your problems?

I have told you this so that my joy might be in you and your joy might be complete. (John 15:11)

What brings joy to your life? You might think of possessions, about certain people in your life, or even certain jobs. These things are fleeting, they come and go. There is one thing that is constant and can always bring you happiness: living in him. He wants you to have complete joy; he created you for it. Joy doesn't come from what you accomplish, your relationships, or what you possess. Complete joy comes from within. Knowing and accepting your own limitations are very freeing. By accepting your shortcomings and acknowledging your weaknesses, your brokenness, you will begin to heal. You will be able to see and focus on the gifts you have been given. Even if you feel lost, God knows where you are, and he has a good future for you. He wants happiness and joy for you. Start a new life today with God and live the days without judging yourself, keeping score or looking back at your failures. His grace, glory, and mercy free you from the past. There is nothing that you can do that will make him leave you; there is no sin too big and no doubt too big. He is always there waiting for you to open your heart and soul to him. Pray to him and give him your brokenness. He accepts you just the way you are, so should you. He wants you to be at peace and feel his love and presence. God is everywhere, so pray anywhere and be happy.

Reflection Questions

1. Do you judge your success in life by the number of things you own?
2. Do you believe that happiness comes from your current circumstances?
3. Do you rely on others to be happy?

> *Fear not, I am with you; be not dismayed; I am your God. I will strengthen you, and help you, and uphold you with my right hand of justice. (Isaiah 41:10)*

You are never alone. God is always with you, and he never abandons you. He is beside you and in front of you. He is waiting in anticipation for you to call his name. Every morning that you wake up, begin your day in prayer. Give thanks for the day and acknowledge that you wish to listen to him and find him among the busyness of the world. Pray with all your heart that the Holy Spirit will guide you through the day. God longs for a relationship with you; he wants to get to know you! You are his creation, and he created you out of love and in His own image. There is only one you in the whole world, and you are perfect in his eyes. He sees your flaws but loves you just the same. He knows every secret, every horrible thing you have thought, done, and said. Yet he loves you so much that he sent his only son to die for you. He is always there; he never abandons you. Whenever you feel alone or lost, look at yourself and your own prayer life. Look back on how you live each day and the choices you made. Ask yourself if you have made God a consistent part of your day. Most likely, it is you that strayed from God and abandoned him. He is all that is good and has unconditional love. Believe and open your heart to him, and he will give you strength and hold you in the palm of his hand.

Reflection Questions

1. Do you love others unconditionally just as Jesus loves you?

2. Why is it so hard to believe God would love you just as you are?

3. How does it make you feel to know that God longs to have a relationship with you?

Not only that, but we even boast of our afflictions, knowing that affliction produces endurance, and endurance, proven character, and proven character, hope, and hope does not disappoint, because the love of God has been poured out into our hearts through the Holy Spirit that has been given to us. (Romans 5:3–4)

Even when you feel hope is gone, remember that God knows your pain and that his promise remains. He promises you eternal salvation. He promises you a life of peace, a life without pain and suffering with him in heaven. This world, this journey, can be harsh, filled with disappointments and falls. When your world is beginning to get dark, then know that you are not fully trusting him. You are traveling on a path away from his light and into the darkness. If you continue down the dark path, you will end up in despair. Turn yourself around and walk toward his light. Get on your knees and pray, read his Word, and spend time alone with him. Sometimes life bombards you with obstacles, and there are so many stressors that you don't feel he is there. Simply take inventory: Have I prayed lately? Have I read the Bible lately? Have I thanked God lately for anything? If you answered no to any of these questions, then it is you that has strayed from God. He wraps himself in light so that when the path is dark, you just have to look around, and you will know which way to turn. When you feel hope is gone, it is then that you need to choose trust over doubt and to "give it up" to God. Offer your pain and your darkness up in prayer. Your struggles are not in vain. They give you character, endurance, and strength. These struggles are a higher calling for you to be closer to him and to have a personal relationship with him.

Reflection Questions

1. When was the last time you opened the Bible, read some of the Gospels, or prayed?

2. Is God the first person you turn to for help when you begin to feel hopeless?

3. What do you do daily that is positive and brings you closer to God?

> *Be still and know that I am God.*
> *(Psalm 46:10)*

Life can get crazy! You have appointments to make, schedules to keep, and errands to run. You have a house to clean, laundry to do, and dishes stacking up in the sink. This is the busyness of the world that consumes you. With all the demands of the world, you find yourself wondering when you have time to spend with God. Here is the thing, there will never be time unless you intentionally schedule a piece of each day to spend with him. Whether it is driving in the car, getting up ten minutes early, or listening to the readings on your phone, intentionally take time out each day. Don't just go through the motions! Read his Word and truly reflect on its meaning and how you can live your life for him. Only in the quietness and stillness will you be able to hear him. Open your heart and be still. God will lead you through whispers. Although his voice resounds for all to hear, you will not hear it through the busyness that consumes you. Keep in contact with him throughout the day. Make time for him and pray, go to your inner room and pray. You will find that being still and quiet is hard because those deadlines creep into your thoughts, or you think that you have "better" things to do than to sit in the quiet and listen. But there is no greater reward than spending time with God. You will find a peace and contentment that you have not known before because it is not of this world but of his.

Reflection Questions

1. Do you set aside time every day to spend with God?

2. Is spending time with God a priority in your life?

3. Is your heart open to hear him, and do you listen for him throughout the day?

4. What part of your day can you intentionally schedule time with him?

ow the Lord is the spirit, and where the spirit of the Lord is, there is freedom. (2 Corinthians 3:17)

Quit punishing yourself for the mistakes you've made. You will never be perfect, so quit striving to be. Only one being walked the earth that was perfect, and his name was Jesus. He was of human form except without sin. He felt every emotion and every pain that you feel. Jesus loves you for who you are, and God made you how he wanted you. God knows you better than you know yourself, so wear your "flaws" with pride and acknowledge your weaknesses. Get down on your knees and pray with all your heart. Ask God to forgive the sins and mistakes you have made. Even if you don't know what to say, close your eyes and just talk to God. There is no wrong way to pray if your heart is open to him. He knows what is in your heart. Ask forgiveness and then listen and feel with your heart. No matter how much you sin or how big your sin is, God will always set you free. God's perfect love and forgiveness will cleanse your soul. Simply believe that he died for your sins, and he will give you eternal life. This is his gift to you, and all you must do is accept it. There is something freeing about forgiveness; you no longer feel like you are being held captive by your own misdoings. Be free, be with God.

Reflection Questions

1. Do you learn from your past mistakes, or do you carry the burden of guilt for them?

2. How is there freedom in admitting your flaws?

3. Do you believe that the mistakes you make define who you are?

> *You too must be patient. Make your hearts firm, because the coming of the Lord is at hand. (James 5:8)*

He is coming! Jesus will come back someday. Your struggles and pain on earth are only temporary, as this earth is just your temporary home. Home is where there is peace and comfort and eternal happiness in heaven. God will wipe away every tear, and there will be no more death, mourning, or pain. That is his promise to you. You can have peace and happiness on earth as well, but this requires you to have an intimate relationship with God and accept that life's trials and tribulations are meant to bring you closer to him. Perfect peace is only something that he can bring. Make sure that you have been meek and humble and not boastful. Your purpose on earth is to have love for all of mankind and treat all equally. It is to be kind and patient and to not judge others. It is to help and serve those in need. These qualities make your heart happy because you are doing God's will. Not only will you be rewarded here on earth, but you will also have a place in heaven with eternal peace. When Jesus does come, be the one in the front saying, "Take me, for I have been a good and faithful servant."

Reflection Questions

1. When Jesus returns, will you be able to say you have lived life to the fullest helping others?

2. Imagine what you will say and do when you see Jesus face-to-face.

3. Do you boast about things you have done, or have you lived life humbly with humility?

And behold, I am with you always, until the end of the age. (Matthew 28:20)

Let God flow through every part of your day not just when there are extraordinary moments but also in the everyday mundane moments. Let him flood all your senses. There is beauty everywhere if you take the time to find it: from the chirp of the robin, to the shy smile of a child, or a glimpse of sunshine peeking out on a dark day. Listen to your heartbeat and know that you are alive and that God created you because he loves you. You are his child, and he gave up his only son for you. Look at things through the eyes of God. See people and places as how God sees them, beautiful and amazing. But don't just see the beauty of God; also act on it. Do the everyday mundane tasks with pride. Do them as if you were doing it for God. Speak to others with kindness and gratitude. Listen to others as if they are the only ones that matter. Speak praises and thanksgiving throughout the day. By keeping God close, you will find that your heart becomes full of gratitude and that life does not seem so grim. A grateful heart can change your attitude and perspective on any situation or ailment. Simply by being with God throughout the day, you will find that life becomes more satisfying and becomes full of his love and grace.

Reflection Questions

1. Are you thankful for the mundane moments of your life?

2. Do you let the busyness of the world clutter your thoughts?

3. When was the last time you just sat in silence and took the time to see the beauty surrounding you?

God is faithful and will not let you be tried beyond your strength; but with the trial he will provide a way out, so that you may be able to bear it. (1 Corinthians 10:13)

There are times you feel defeated and life knocks you to the ground. You may doubt you can get back up or go any further. During those times, think of Jesus and how He fell carrying the very cross he was to be crucified on. He got back up every time. He carried a three-hundred-pound cross for you so that you could go to heaven. He had people laughing at him, spitting on him, crowning him with thorns, and casting lots for his clothes. He accepted that it was his Father's will. He was to die. When you fall, remember Jesus's perseverance and gain strength through him, knowing that he died on that cross for you. He will always be there to pick you up. Pray for his will and trust the path he has given you and accept it without hesitation. Be obedient, as he is a loving father that only wants what's best for you. He knows your future. He knows what needs to happen to fulfill his perfect plan for your life. Although you may never understand the whys or the "How come?" you must give him thanks for his perfect love. Life isn't always easy, but he will give you the strength to face your struggles. Remember, it is not how strong you are but how strong Jesus is. God is faithful and will never abandon you. With each trial in life you face, the strength of God is within you.

Reflection Questions

1. How you will be stronger because of your struggles?

2. Would anyone else you know suffer the humiliation Jesus did for you?

3. When was the last time you thanked him for what you are going through?

> *For by grace you have been saved through faith, and this is not from you; it is the gift of God. (Ephesians 2:8)*

Do you believe that you are not good enough for God? Do you feel guilty about the past decisions you have made? Do you think you have made too many mistakes that God couldn't possibly love you? Well, here is the good news! He is a loving and forgiving God. Instead of doubting, bask in his mercy. It is his gift to you, and all you must do is accept it. Believe with all your heart that Jesus died for your sins and ask for forgiveness for all those mistakes. He *will* forgive you. He will rinse you clean. He not only forgives but also forgets. Only you confine yourself to the chains of past, but he can set you free. You can be free from your past and be born again, cleansed from sin. Your afflictions of guilt for your past choices do not define you. God does not judge you, as all humans are sinners. You can have a wonderful future ahead of you with Jesus's healing and redemption. He can create a better you if you follow him. His forgiveness can give you a sense of peace. He sees the good in you when nobody else can. He can make something beautiful out of you. Believe in your heart and speak with your mouth that God is your salvation. With this newfound grace, you must also forgive those that have sinned against you. Jesus did not come for the righteous ones but for the sinners. He came for you. He died for you, a sinner, so that your sins can be forgiven and you can have eternal peace with God in heaven.

Reflection Questions

1. God forgives and forgets, so why is it so hard for you to do the same?

2. When was the last time you have looked within and found the good qualities God sees in you?

3. Do you feel unworthy of his forgiveness? It is always there, only you can reject it.

Life can be scary. You might be afraid to face the day because of your circumstances or limitations, afraid you will make a mistake or that you won't be able to handle anything else going wrong. Conflict at some point is inevitable. Tasks where you feel out of control will happen; it is not within your power to control every aspect of your circumstances. If you live your life in fear, you will miss the wondrous gifts that he has given you. Eventually, that fear will paralyze you, and your world will become small and dark. The very life that God wanted you to enjoy will make you feel smothered and trapped. But God says, "Fear not, I will help you." Trust him that he is there to help you face your daily struggles. It is not hard to have faith when the days are going smooth. Faith is when you are afraid and feel out of control and you still trust him. He will lead you in the right direction to help you through that stressful moment. Pray to him and give your problems up to him, and he will help. Then give thanks to him and focus on the things you are grateful for. Make him the center of your life. Giving him control will make your fears grow dimmer because he is holding your hand. Walk with him, and your fears will no longer paralyze you, and you can face any problems you might encounter. God is in control, so you don't have to be.

Reflection Questions

1. What fears prevent you from enjoying life and being at peace?

2. Have you accepted your limitations or circumstances, and what do you think of yourself because of them?

3. Have you given thanks to God that you are given the opportunity through your fears to grow closer to him?

Blessed are the meek, for they shall inherit the land. (Matthew 5:5)

Jesus came to serve, not to be served. This should also be the purpose of your life, to serve. Your focus should not be on yourself or your material possessions. You should not be boastful and brag on your accomplishments, for that is not how success is measured. Jesus was not boastful; at times, he told those that he healed to not speak of what he did. Be aware of your actions and words. Ask yourself, "If Jesus was by my side, would he be proud of what I did or the words that came from my mouth?" Jesus was humble, and even washed the feet of his own disciples. He spoke to those who were forbidden and helped those whom others did not deem worthy. He followed God's commandments and obeyed his Father's will. Jesus knew that he was to die on that cross. He could have asked to be saved and spared from crucifixion, as the angels were waiting to help him, yet he did not. He knew it was God's will for him to die for our sins, and he obeyed. Just as he served others while he walked the earth, you are called to serve as well. You are to be patient, kind, meek, and humble. If you see someone naked, then clothe him. If you see someone hungry, then feed him. If you see someone thirsty, then give him drink. If you see someone ill, then care for him. If you see a stranger, then welcome him. Just as Jesus did these, so should you.

Reflection Questions

1. When was the last time you truly went out of your way to help those in need?

2. Look around your community, there are people hurting everywhere. Have you taken the time to look for the broken?

3. Are you boastful and brag to others, or are you humble?

This is the day the Lord has made; let us rejoice and be glad in it. (Psalm 118:24)

Each day is a gift from God. Every day you wake up is another day for a second chance. It is a chance to refuel your soul. The difference between a good day and a bad day is your amount of faith. Take note of all the little wonderful things. Find the breathtaking moments of the day, and don't focus on everything that has gone wrong. Those closed doors were closed for a reason and may lead to new exciting paths. Every night think to yourself, *Do I have any regrets? Did I tell everyone I know I love them? Did foul words come out of my mouth? Did my actions make God proud?* Each day may be your last, so don't spend it mad at yesterday. Don't let the broken pieces of yesterday guide your today. By waking up with the grace of God, you have an opportunity to make today amazing. Make every little thing you do amazing. No matter the most menial task, do it with love and the intention of Jesus. Do it for Jesus, and he will see what is in your heart, and you will be rewarded with his unconditional love, extraordinary mercy, and eternal peace.

Reflection Questions

1. Do you start your day with prayer and thanksgiving?

2. Check your attitude. Do you find that you see the negative throughout the day and not the positive?

3. When was the last time you noticed the sunrise, the sunset, or the beauty of nature surrounding you?

> *ray without ceasing. In all cir-
> cumstances give thanks, for this is
> the will of God for you in Christ Jesus. (1
> Thessalonians 5:17–18)*

Life is not always fair. Some days you will feel like nothing is going your way. There will be disappointments and heartache along the way. At times, others treat you poorly, your feelings get hurt, and you may even feel down and abandoned. It is during those times when God wants you to grow from the adversity. He knows every decision you make and every challenge you face. When you begin to feel all alone and question why you must endure your struggles, you are trying to face life on your own and not with God. Pray to the Holy Spirit to give you direction, strength, and wisdom. God is always there, always listening, and always loving. When your prayers go unanswered and you have disappointments in life, then it is God's will. He knows what is best for you and wants you to be closer to him. Be thankful for the blessings that you do have. He wants you to trust and believe in him. Just as when we pray "The Lord's Prayer," "Thy kingdom come, thy will be done, on earth as it is in heaven." Whatever challenges you are facing, know that you will get through it. Pray, listen, and give thanks. You may never understand God's will but know that God is good and that he loves you. God knows your journey, so no matter what circumstances life may bring, be thankful and pray for his peace and strength. Trust him. For God's plan is perfect for you, even if you don't understand.

Reflection Questions

1. Mindfully say the words to "The Lord's Prayer." What do they mean to you?

2. Do you blame God for all the disappointments in your life, or do you take responsibility for your choices?

3. Do you use your limitations as excuses when things don't go your way?

> *My love shall never leave you nor my covenant of peace be shaken, says the Lord, who has mercy on you. (Isaiah 54:10)*

Life can be a struggle. There are days you question the purpose of being here on earth. Your negative thoughts overtake you and you wonder how you are going to trudge through another day. You may even tell yourself, *I can't do it*, and feel useless or worthless. Even when you doubt yourself or doubt God, his love is still there. He loves you unconditionally despite your doubts. Even when you make bad choices, he still loves you. He longs to have a relationship with you. You see, happiness is a choice. Even under the bleakest circumstances, you can choose to be happy by accepting that this is his plan for you. Happiness is knowing that despite your everyday flaws, he loves you and forgives you. Happiness is waking up in the morning knowing that each day is a new day to spend time with him. Every morning, know that his mercy is new. Take the time to be thankful, for a grateful heart is a happy heart. He will always give you the strength you need to get through any situation. Trust him and seek him. God will never withhold his love from you, as he loves you unconditionally. Happiness is knowing that he is your shield who will help you not give way to negativity. When you follow him, your heart will be full of happiness and peace.

Reflection Questions

1. Do you believe that your circumstances dictate your happiness?

2. What are three good things that happened to you today?

3. When was the last time you opened your eyes and thanked God for the mere fact that you woke up to another day?

But seek first the kingdom of God and his righteousness, and all these things will be given you besides. Do not worry about tomorrow; tomorrow will take care of itself. (Matthew 6:33–34)

We all worry from time to time, but worry can turn into anxiety, and this emotion will consume you. You may worry about finances, your kids, conflicts with others, or even your health. Thinking of what will happen tomorrow is wasteful energy. He has given you the precious gift of the now, this very moment, to enjoy. Live in the present and cherish all the beauty and gifts that he has surrounded you with. Look at someone and see them again for the first time, listen to the birds, or admire his handiwork of the sunrise. Worrying about tomorrow causes anxiety and takes away today's peace. It robs you of what he ultimately wants for you— peace and happiness. Anxiety is when you live in the future, but remember you don't have to worry because he is already there taking care of it. Tomorrow is not within your control, but the here and now are, so be thankful for what you have. Today praise him, read his Word, and listen, as God is in control. Choose him as you go through your day, and you will find that you worry less. Every decision you make through the day reflects who you are. By making choices that reflect him, you know that it is right and worries diminish. He is already taking care of you and your future, so trust him and be thankful for the here and now. As the saying goes, "None of us know what tomorrow holds, but know that he holds the tomorrow."

Reflection Questions

1. How much time do you spend a day worrying about what will happen in the future?

2. Does anxiety consume you? Then work on trusting God and his perfect plan for you.

3. Do you make choices that you are proud of and you know are the "right" things to do?

Because if you confess with your mouth that Jesus is Lord and believe in your heart that God raised him from the dead you will be saved. For with the heart one believes and is justified and with the mouths ones confesses and is saved. (Roman 10:9–10)

We are all broken people. If you think that you aren't good enough for him, you are wrong. He loves us all: from the child still in the womb to the oldest of old and everyone in between. No one who walks the earth is perfect and without sin except for Jesus. He knows that you can never be like him. Without him, you would never achieve salvation and enter the kingdom of God. You don't have to do anything magnificent or grand, just live simply and humbly and admit your sins to him. Believe in your heart that he died for you so that your sins can be forgiven. If you think that you don't deserve his grace because of past choices and actions, you are mistaken. Jesus not only forgives but also forgets. Jesus is already there, and you are already saved. The spiritual battle has already been won, so claim your victory. The only way you are not saved is if you reject his gift. We are all worthy of the cross if we believe in him. Being saved doesn't come with stipulations. It doesn't say you are only worthy if you have done this many deeds or only sinned so many times. He says that he loves you unconditionally no matter who you are and what you have done. His love is perfect and pure, and there is no one else that can promise that.

Reflection Questions

1. In what way do you think you are too broken for God?

2. If you reject his gift of salvation, then why?

3. How does it feel to know that someone loves you know matter how broken you are?

So faith, hope, love remain, these three; but the greatest of these is love. (1 Corinthians 13:13)

How many times a day do you put yourself down for your flaws and weaknesses? Or maybe you think that you are "above" certain classes and better than others. God created each and every one of us the same...in his image. God made you just the way you are. He created every flaw and every imperfection you have. Be kind to yourself, for you are just what he created. He wants to be close to you through your imperfections. He wants you to be humble and not be judgmental of yourself or others. He wants you to love yourself and others just as he loves us. Your flaws and experiences help mold you so you can see each other's struggles. You can emphasize and sympathize with others and follow in his footsteps and love "the least of these." You can love others and give them hope by letting them know that Jesus is there for them every second of the day. He loves you and all mankind so much that he died for you so that your sins can be forgiven and you can have eternal peace. That is pure love, so listen to his calling to you and answer him by loving one another and loving yourself.

Reflection Questions

1. Do you love yourself, flaws and all?
2. What does it feel like to know he died just for you so that you can go to heaven?
3. Do you often find yourself judging others by their appearance, status, etc. instead of seeing them through the eyes of God?

> *He gives strength to the fainting; for the weak he makes vigor abound. Though young men faint and grow weary, and youths stagger and fall, they that hope in the Lord will renew their strength, they will soar as with eagles' wings; they will run and not grow weary, walk and not grow faint. (Isaiah 40:29–31)*

Some days your heart and soul are tired, and it is hard to get through the day. You feel like you're drowning and want to crawl back in bed, pull the covers over your head, and say, "I give up." Life can get overwhelming fast, so learn to lean on him and rely on him. Humbly ask him to give you strength to carry on. Unfortunately, life moves on, even if you don't want it to. You should keep things in perspective and remember the battle is not yours but God's. Give up complete control to him so that he can fight the battle for you. Put your life in his hands and trust him. Pray for strength and courage to continue the path he is leading you. He is in control, and he knows the path for you. Even if you feel like you may stumble on the path, take that first step of faith, and he will light your way. His love is perfect. All your struggles will be worth it when you are in the kingdom of heaven where peace prevails and all suffering and pain are gone. Remember that this earthly dwelling is not your home. The path you travel down makes you who you are, and every battle makes you stronger in faith. If you turn to him in your time of need, He will be your strength and your stronghold.

Reflection Questions

1. Do you give up your problems to him when you feel overwhelmed?

2. When was the last time you got down on your knees and prayed for strength?

3. Do you read his words through the Bible, devotional, etc. to find comfort?

> *For I know well the plans I have in mind for you, says the Lord, plans for your welfare, not for woe! Plans to give you a future full of hope. When you call me, when you go to pray to me, I will listen to you. (Jeremiah 29:11–12)*

There will be days when life is falling apart. Your circumstances may seem bleak, and you are afraid nothing will get better. There may always be turmoil around you, but pray and ask him to calm the storm, just like that day Jesus and his disciples were at sea. Jesus fell asleep, and despite the storm, he did not wake. The disciples were afraid and woke him and asked that he calm the storm, and he did. He will not always calm the raging storm but instead give you the strength to carry on in the midst of the storm. Whichever he decides, remember that God doesn't just have a plan for you; he has the perfect plan. If you are going through struggles, it is because you are supposed to. He is calling you to come closer to him through those hardships. Life will never be perfect, but peace and contentment within are possible. Your daily challenges can help you find peace inside. Let him know that you are willing to build a relationship with him. There will be times you won't understand the purpose of the path you are on, but you must trust him. During this difficult time, say, "I trust you, Lord." These words are powerful because no matter what the outcome, you are relying on him to keep you afloat during the storm.

Reflection Questions

1. What can you do to show that you truly trust him that he has the perfect plan for you?

2. How can your struggles bring you closer to God?

3. What would peace feel like to you?

Your kingdom come, your will be done, on earth as in heaven. (Matthew 6:10)

What is faith? It is defined as a strong belief or trust, but it goes much deeper than that. Faith is believing in God when you realize your unanswered prayers. Faith is believing that he is loving and merciful despite your struggles. It is not deserting him when life gets hard, just like he doesn't desert you. Faith is putting your life in his hands and trusting him. God is not a servant who is to answer your every request; this puts you in charge. Faith is believing he is there during your most treacherous storms and trusting him that the outcome is his will. Even if you don't understand it or like it, you still need to be grateful and thankful during those storms. Remember those gifts that you have, even if they are hard to see through the pouring rain. Be thankful for the gift of him and that he is loving and walks alongside of you. Even when your faith is the weakest and you are afraid, he does not give up on you, and he loves you unconditionally, flaws and all. Faith is in your heart, and you can't just have it when it is convenient for you. Be vigilant and make time with him. During our hardest moments, our faith should be the strongest; however, at times, it is the weakest. He wants to know you and will love you without condition. Give him control and humbly say your prayers and trust him no matter what the circumstances.

Reflection Questions

1. How can you improve your prayer life?

2. What does faith mean to you?

3. Even though you may not understand unanswered prayers, do you still have a grateful heart?

P eace I leave with you; my peace I give to you. Not as the world gives do I give it you. Do not let your hearts be troubled or afraid. (John 14:27)

If you let it, fear will consume you and will paralyze you. Maybe it is the fear of how you are going to cope through the day, the fear of not knowing what is to come, or the fear of whether or not you will recover. But fear can rob you of enjoying the life that God made for you. It will smother out any light and hope that you have, and darkness will consume you. Fear can make your world small and dark. Trust in him and do not be afraid. Take that energy you use on the worry and fear and praise God. Have a grateful and thankful heart that he is giving you the opportunity to rely on him. He wants to draw you closer to him. Being self-sufficient is not what he wants; he wants you to solely rely on him. By giving up control and giving up the fear to him, you can be free from this burden. A peaceful heart will consume you, a peace you have not felt before. He has loved you before you were even created and desires you to have peace when you are troubled and afraid. With peace comes hope, with hope comes light, with light comes God, and with God comes healing.

Reflection Questions

1. What things in life do you fear the most, and how can you give them up to God?

2. How can you use the energy of your fear in a positive way?

3. How can you be the light for someone else who is sharing the same fears as you?

> *Have no anxiety at all, but in everything, by prayer and petition, with thanksgiving, make your requests known to God. Then the peace of God that surpasses all understanding will guard your hearts and minds in Christ Jesus. (Philippians 4:6–7)*

Live in this moment, don't relive the past or worry about the future. Anxiety will consume you if you look to the future. You become anxious about how to face each day ahead and anxious about what the days ahead may bring. Anxiety can completely overwhelm you because you cannot control your circumstances. When you are overcome by anxiety, then you are doubting God. Your very actions say that you don't trust him. Focus on today because God has taken care of your tomorrows. Thank him for that exact moment you are in because in the present is where you find peace in him. When you trust him with your tomorrows, having a thankful heart, your anxiety will subside. He wants you to be thankful each day that he has given you life and thankful despite your struggles. Through his Word, he tells you to not look forward, as he is already there. You need to continue to have faith in him and continue to believe that he will heal your soul and banish your anxiety. Give your anxiety up to him. Even if your physical or mental ailments do not fully heal, you will be spiritually healed. He will help you accept any limitations. He asks that you make your requests known to him, and if it is his will, that request will be granted. If not, then he will grant you the peace and strength to carry on despite your struggles. Live in the present moment with gratitude and keep your focus on him throughout the day, and you will see that he is a good and gracious God.

Reflection Questions

1. How do you let anxiety consume your life?

2. Even though you have daily struggles, there are always things to be grateful for. Can you find them throughout the day?

3. Can you identify the things that are in your control? And for the ones that aren't, can you then give them up to God?

*K*now that the Lord does wonders for his faithful one; the Lord will hear when me when I call upon him. (Psalm 4:4)

When you feel down and depressed, it is easy to lose faith and feel overwhelmed with life. You may struggle with daily tasks like getting out of bed because you don't want to face today's problems. Your days may seem dark because you feel he has abandoned you when you need him the most. Sometimes it is hard to see his light when you are in the shadows, so you must let go and have faith. It's hard to "let go and let God." You want to feel as if you have control over life, but ironically, giving up control to God and putting your hardship in God's hands are very freeing and give you peace. Know that he loves you, has given his life, and is walking by your side. If you can't feel him, then you need to be alone with him. Make time out of your busy day and sit and meditate. Listen to him as he is talking to you. Busyness tends to consume us all and distracts us, so we just don't listen. You should be open and let him in. If you make quiet time daily with the Lord, he will hear you call, and you'll find that trust and faith come easier. A calm and peace take over your heart and your mind. It helps you keep your situation in perspective and to realize that any adverse circumstances are actually opportunities for you to grow closer to him.

Reflection Questions

1. What can you do differently throughout the day so that you can listen and hear him?

2. What do you need to do to get out of the shadows and see his light?

3. Why is it so hard to have faith during difficult times?

Guide me in your truth and teach me, for you are God my Savior, and for you I wait all the day. (Psalm 25:5)

Are you lost and feel that God has abandoned you? If you do, your days are probably dark. You feel hopeless and helpless and wonder why he has abandoned you in your most critical time of need. You think, how could he not see how badly you were hurting, and why didn't he care enough to hold out his hand and say, "Come, I am here"? Here is the thing—he *was* holding out his hand, but *you* just weren't listening. He didn't stop trying; it was you that stopped looking up and reaching out. Hopelessness clouds your judgment, and you will find that it is easier to look down in the dark instead of falling on your knees and looking up. He has been beside you the whole time and has felt your every heartache and every pain. He walked it first and knows your pain and has shown you that hope can rise again from the grave. When you become hopeless, you begin to think you are not good enough or worthy enough for God. You feel down on yourself and you think that he could not love you with all your doubts. Truth is...God loves you, flaws and all. He will always love you for who you are, and he will always love you for who you will be.

Reflection Questions

1. What traits about yourself do you feel Jesus couldn't love?

2. What times in your life have you stopped caring and found yourself doubting and feeling lost?

3. Do you pray daily for strength and trust him enough to hold out your hand when you feel hopeless?

The Lord, your God, is in your midst, a mighty Savior; he will rejoice over you with gladness and renew you in his love, he will sing joyfully because of you. (Zephaniah 3:17)

God loves broken people. He loves all of us: those of us who are full of anger or fear, those of us who suffer from mental disorders, those who suffer from physical illness, those of us who make mistakes and have regrets. We are all broken, and God loves us exactly the way we are. He uses all our broken pieces to make something beautiful. He rejoices over you, as you are his creation. He is the glue that can make our life fulfilling and worthwhile. He is the one that can give us peace and hope. He is the one who makes us thankful for being broken. Without our brokenness, we would have never called out to him, never would have found him, and never would have given our life to him. He is what makes us whole and fills all the holes and cracks to make us one with him. We need to know that without him, we will continue to break into smaller pieces. Listen to him as he sings joyfully when you believe in him. Remember that God is greater than the burdens we are carrying and that he can make us whole and give us peace.

Reflection Questions

1. In what way can your brokenness bring you closer to God?

2. What pieces of your life do you feel need "put together" the most?

3. What will it take before you put all your trust in God?

> *Trust in the Lord with all your heart, on your own intelligence rely not; in all your ways be mindful of him, and he will make straight your paths. (Proverbs 3:5–6)*

Trust him through the heartache, trust him through the pain, and trust him with your life. There will be times when you feel like your life is spinning out of control and you feel helpless. You may feel like you have nowhere to turn and nothing helps. These are the times you are not trusting God. You have decided that you wanted to be in control and not him and took your life back into your own hands. When trying to be self-sufficient is when you are the most powerless. You are not listening to him and the path you are to take, you are listening to the world. When you give your life over to God and say, "I trust you," a burden will be lifted off you. He has a perfect plan for you, and though you may not understand his wisdom, know it is his will for you. His steadfast love cannot be denied, and he will love you throughout the ages and through the storms in your life. He understands every struggle you go through and provides hope to those who believe. His compassion is so deep and is beyond words. There is no one more trustworthy than he, so trust him with your life and your heart, and he will not lead you astray.

Reflection Questions

1. Why is it so hard to trust God?
2. What happens when you try to control all the circumstances around you?
3. What is the first step you can take to give up control to God and not fully rely on yourself?

*F*aith is the realization of what is hoped for and evidence of things not seen. (Hebrews 11:1)

You must be firm in your faith to stand firm. Faith doesn't come easily. It comes with struggles and doubt and "dark" nights. But these are necessary for your faith to grow. For in those dark stormy moments is when your faith is truly tested. It is easy to doubt he is there, and you begin to lose your way in the dark. Faith is knowing that he is always there, even when you can't feel him. Without faith, you will waiver in your beliefs and your hope. You will not be able to stand strong when life becomes difficult. The days you don't feel he is there, make sure that your heart and mind are open. Listen for him throughout the day, for it does not matter how strong you are but rather how strong God is. Faith will not change your circumstances, but it makes them seem possible to handle. He has a plan for you, and you should trust him enough to put your life in his hands. You may never understand his reason, but you must trust his will and realize there is a purpose to your journey.

Reflection Questions

1. How do you live in accordance to the values of Jesus?

2. Do you tend to give up easily when life challenges you or do you use the strength of God to help you through?

3. How have those "dark" nights made you grow in your faith?

Come to me, all you who labor and are burdened, and I will give you rest. (Matthew 11:28–30)

Rest in the Lord. When you feel that life is spinning out of control, rest in him. The noise and busyness of the world can make you weary, and you don't have time to catch your breath. But make the time and take the time to breathe in the Lord. Just be with him, take deep cleansing breaths, and clear your mind. Don't think of everything on your to-do list but rather clear your mind and think of the absence of something. Focus on every breath going in and going out. Be thankful for each breath and clear your mind of only him. Just sit and be with him. Imagine what it would be like if you were to meet Jesus on earth. Look at the beauty around you and the sounds you hear. When imagining this, notice the incredible peace and love you feel. He longs for you to spend time with him. Listen to the quiet of your heart and don't let the busyness of the world sneak in. As you slowly breathe him in, feel his calming presence. Just rest in him and be with him.

Reflection Questions

1. What would Jesus do and say to you when he comes to you?

2. Why is it so hard to clear your mind and only think of him?

3. How does relaxing in him change your perspective on all the busyness of life?

Therefore, put on the armor of God, that you may be able to resist on the evil day and, having done everything, to hold your ground. In all circumstances, hold faith as a shield, to quench all the flaming arrows of the evil one. (Ephesians 6:13, 16)

You may feel unworthy of him. You wonder if you have not done enough good in this world to deserve his mercy and love. Fact is, Jesus walked the earth and died for you knowing that you do wrong. We are all sinners. Jesus was among us and knows all the evil and injustice in the world, yet he still chose death to save us. He, above all, knows the temptations of the world and how easy it is to make choices that do not align with God. The world is filled with evil trying to get you to doubt God or make you become bitter because of your struggles. But those feelings are not ones that God wants for you. He wants you to feel his peace and forgiveness. Put on your shield of armor so that you may resist temptation through the day. As you are faced with choices, acknowledge him and what his choice would be and follow him. Follow in your heart what you know is "right," and this will keep you free from the evil one. Walk in his footsteps, and you will feel his loving arms wrap around you while he protects and guides you through the day.

Reflection Questions

1. What are the hard choices you face through the day that don't align with God?

2. Do you put yourself in situations where it is hard to follow in his footsteps?

3. Do you find yourself repeating sins, or do you learn from them?

Ah, Lord God, you have made heaven and earth by your great might, with your outstretched arm; nothing is impossible to you. (Jeremiah 32:17)

Living, he loved you; dying, he saved you. He can save you from your own self-destructive thoughts. Doubting yourself and the path that you are on can be crippling. Soon negative thoughts can turn into negative actions, which only confirms the self-doubt. You might even have thoughts of not being worthy of his grace. Remember, though, that his grace is stronger than the negative in you. Your imperfections will not override God's promises. As Marianne Williamson wrote, "Until we have met the monsters in ourselves, we keep trying to slay them in the outer world. And we find that we cannot. For all darkness in the world stems from darkness in the heart. And it is there that we must do our work". In an ever-changing world, he is the only thing that is constant and unwavering. When your world turns dark and your heart becomes heavy, remember to look up.

He will be there to bring light to your heart. You are truly blessed because God's strength is your weapon to defeat the doubt. God is bigger than your past pain, anger, fears, and scars of this world. He is your weapon to turn these past hurts into healing.

Reflection Questions

1. What darkness is in your heart that you need to overcome?

2. How does self-doubt effect your relationship with God?

3. How do the scars on Jesus's hand begin your healing?

> *Examine yourselves to see whether you are living in faith. Test yourselves. Do you not realize that Jesus Christ is in you? (2 Corinthians 13:5)*

God should be the first you think of when you wake up in the morning. Your relationship with him should take first priority in your life. Not even your family and friends should come before God. You will find that serving God will make you a better person, and in return you can be a better parent to your kids, a better relative to your family, and a better friend to others. Stop and take inventory if you are living in faith. Do you seek his assistance during stressful situations? Do you make it a priority to reach out to others in need? Do you pray for guidance? But most importantly, do you thank God for your blessings and the struggles that make your stronger? Look for the little blessings that you receive throughout the day and be thankful for them. Look to see if you take all the "basics" for granted, like the mere fact you woke to take another breath or live in a country where you are free to worship God. Getting back to the basics of life will give you new perspective about what is important and how much you have to be thankful for. A thankful heart makes a faithful heart. It shows that you trust in him and that every day you will do your best to live in faith.

Reflection Questions

1. Do the decisions you make throughout the day show that you are living in faith?

2. What "basics" are you thankful for every day?

3. Do you pass or fail the "tests" you have throughout the day?

> *ut I will call upon God, and the Lord will save me. In the evening, and at dawn, and at noon, I will grieve and moan, and he will hear my voice. (Psalm 55:17–18)*

What a friend you have in Jesus. He is always there whenever you call his name, day or night. He can take away your worries and your fears. He can relieve your heartbreak and loneliness. He is always listening and knows what is on your heart before you do. He has more faith in you than you do and loves you unconditionally no matter what mistakes you have made. In his eyes, you are perfect in every way despite your flaws. He forgives and then forgets. He knows what struggles you bear and wants to be the one to ease them. He never leaves your side no matter how many times you try to push him away. He listens when you talk and cries when you cry. You don't have to shout or cry out loud because he hears even the silent cry. He wants to have a relationship with you. Just believe in him, and he will give you the ultimate gift of eternal peace. Have a thankful heart and talk to him throughout the day. Tell him your worries and your fears. Pray fervently every day. But most importantly, take time to sit in quiet with him and listen, for he will be there…waiting. He is proud that you are his, and you will have a friend forever, knowing that you are a child of God.

Reflection Questions

1. How does it make you feel that he believes you are perfect despite your flaws?

2. What are some characteristics about yourself that you can improve on?

3. Are you a friend to others as Jesus is a friend to you?

The favors of the Lord are not exhausted, his mercies are not spent; they are renewed each morning, so great is his faithfulness. (Lamentations 3:22–23)

His mercy is new every morning, so all your negative thoughts or bad choices of the day before have been forgiven. Every morning is a new day to do better, to better serve God by loving others and lending a helping hand. Through service to others, you can find refuge. Give yourself a chance to be who God created you to be. God created each of us for greatness. This doesn't mean we must do great things but to live each day greatly. Live in each moment and don't let the past prevent you from seeing how wonderful you are, for you were created in his image. Living in the past can only bring you regret and sadness. Don't let the future cause you anxiety, for it will rob you of enjoying that moment. Now is a moment that you will never get back, so live each moment and love each moment. Listen to his tender whispers of love, as each day you open your eyes is his gift to you. He has given you the gift of mercy and forgiveness, and all you have to do is accept it. None of us deserves his mercy, but he gives it to us anyway.

Reflection Questions

1. In what ways can you live each day greatly?
2. Do you live in the present, or do you find yourself thinking about the past or the future?
3. How does it make you feel to know God loves you enough to give you new mercy each new morning?

I am the way and the truth and the life. No one comes to the Father except through me. (John 14:6)

He is the way, the truth, and the life. Who else can say that? When you follow him, you follow truth. You will never be in the dark no matter how horrible your circumstances are. In life, there will be many people and ideas that will try to detour you and distract you from following him. But remember, he is the only way. He is the only way to true happiness and fulfillment. You must surrender your life to him, and he will turn chaos into order. No matter how many temptations you face through the day or how many demons haunt your past, he is waiting for you to take his hand so he can guide you. He will give you peace, contentment, and happiness in this world that is filled with pain, cruelty, fear, and anxiety. You can thrive, and not just survive, by saying two little words. These words can change your life and give you a life of freedom. Surrender control to God and say, "I'm yours." Bow down in humility and faith, and he will hear your cry. Life doesn't have to be hard, as Jesus is an invitation to simplicity. He knows what is best for you and knows your request before you do. He will never lead you astray, so follow him and his teachings, and the path you take will always be filled with light.

Reflection Questions

1. What wrong paths have you taken in life, and how can you learn from them?

2. When you tell God, "I'm yours," what do you mean by it?

3. What distractions do you have that prevent you from following God?

By waiting and by calm you shall be saved, in quiet and in trust your strength lies. (Isaiah 30:15)

Sometimes you must wait and listen. Have patience in the world and spend quiet time with God every day. You will hear him in the silence. Listen to him with your heart and feel him with your soul. Pray to him daily for your requests but know that everything will happen in his time in accordance with his will. He is always listening to your prayers and always listening to what's in your heart. Trust in him and lean on him, and he will heal your spirit. As you spiritually heal, you will find the physical and mental anguish you experience diminishes. With spiritual healing comes peace and strength, even when your prayers go unanswered. Don't get frustrated and give up prayer because you think he's not with you. Continue to devote time to him and faith in him. The more you give up control to him, you will find peace despite your daily struggles and hardships. He will hold you in the palm of his hands, and a calm will envelop you as you wait in his glory.

Reflection Questions

1. When spending time in quiet, do you truly listen for him?

2. What can you do to take the first step to spiritually heal?

3. What unanswered prayers have there been that you have been grateful for?

I command you: be firm and stead-fast! Do not fear nor be dismayed, for the Lord, your God, is with you wherever you go. (Joshua 1:9)

When you feel afraid and like the weight of the world is on your shoulders, be brave, as there is power in the name of Jesus. You can be a warrior to fight against the hardships of your life. His power and strength can hold you as he protects and guides you. God has his armies of angels watching and protecting you. This should fill you with courage to know that you have the strength of many. Courage is a wonderful gift from the Holy Spirit that will help you know what is "right" and give you the confidence to face the world. It is so easy to be afraid of all the darkness in this world. Focus on something bigger than yourself; focus on God as he takes away the fear. When you bask in his light, the world seems doable, and your fear slowly fades. He can make you brave, and you can be strong. Jesus faced ridicule, pain, and betrayal for you. He was brave hanging on that cross as he died for you. He died so that your sins can be forgiven and you can have eternal life. Jesus conquered death by rising up on the third day. There is no greater power and no one braver than Jesus. Let his example give you courage and confidence to face each day and live your life fully.

Reflection Questions

1. How does the Holy Spirit guide you through the day?

2. In what ways can you be brave?

3. What kind of strength and courage would it take to die for someone else's sins?

About the Author

Terri was raised in Victoria, a small rural community in western Kansas. She married her high school sweetheart, and together they have two teenage boys. She attended Fort Hays State University and graduated with a BS in psychology. For over twenty years, she has worked at the local mental health center where she found her passion working with the severely and persistently mentally ill.